A FREELANCER'S GUIDE TO FREELANCING

AN INTRODUCTION ON THE PROFITABLE LIFESTYLE OF FREELANCING

FRANCOIS HENSLEY

CONTENTS

Title Page	1
INTRODUCTION	5
WHAT IS FREELANCING?	7
ADVANTAGES OF FREELANCING	10
THE DISADVANTAGES OF FREELANCING	14
GETTING STARTED AS A FREELANCER	17
WHAT YOU NEED TO KNOW ABOUT FREELANCING	20
BEST WEBSITES FOR GENERAL FREELANCE SERVICES	23
BEST WEBSITES FOR GRAPHICS DESIGNER FREELANCE SERVICES	26
BEST PLATFORMS FOR WEBSITE AND SOFTWARE DEVELOPING SERVICES	28
BEST PLATFORMS FOR CUSTOMER SUPPORT SERVICES	30
BEST PLATFORMS FOR MARKETERS	31
THE BEST PLATFORMS FOR VIDEO EDITING SERVICES	33
THE BEST PLATFORMS FOR SALES	35
THE BEST PLATFORMS FOR PHOTOGRAPHER SERVICES	37
THE BEST WEBSITES FOR WRITING FREELANCE JOBS	40
THE BEST WEBSITES FOR VIRTUAL ASSISTANTS	43
CONCLUSION	46

INTRODUCTION

So, you want to become a freelancer? Perhaps you are considering freelance because it is a fast, convenient and easily affordable way to start earning an income from home. Perhaps you want to do this on the side, even as you work on your regular job every day. Perhaps you want to venture into freelancing as a way to generate extra income in order to save for that big-ticket item you've always wanted or to pay off your creditcard.

Whatever your reason for considering freelance, you won't find a material as helpful for beginner freelancers as this book is. Coming from a place of personal experience, I have put together all the information I know about freelancing into this book you hold in your hand.

We will first define freelancing, then delve into the benefits that freelancing offers. We will also examine the disadvantages of freelancing. And when we are done with these basics, we will discuss the seven crucial keys to getting started as a freelancer.

We will discuss all that you need to know about freelancing; from filing your taxes as an independent contractor, to getting paid in full and on time, to dealing with your health insurance, retirement plan and other benefits; and to exploring the online world of freelancing and the opportunities it offers you.

You will also get an exhaustive list with detailed descriptions of some of the most popular online freelance marketplaces right now. I also include information on how to get registered and started as a freelancer on these platforms.

Freelancing allows for greater independence over a job; allows you to work on a part time basis if you don't want to leave your nine-to-five just yet; allows you to be your own boss; and offers a whole host of other benefits.

It is my hope that by the time you are done reading this book, you will have a better idea on what freelancing is and be fired up to go out and become the very best freelancer that you can be.

WHAT IS FREELANCING?

The meaning of freelancing is very straightforward, and it is defined as the process through which a self-employed individual makes his services available to clients who pay for his expertise and experience at a mutually agreed upon rate. A freelancer is not considered an employee of his client.

It is a unique way of working that is steadily gaining ground in the United States, as well as other countries of the world. Forbes Magazine records and reports that more than 57 million Americans freelanced in one capacity or the other in 2017, and projects that this figure might reach more than a 100 million Americans by 2027. With many more people worldwide.

Freelancing is unique because the person involved (freelancer) is not employed by any specific company and does not necessarily have a specific job title. Yet, he can apply for and get jobs from a variety of sources, meaning that he can have more than one client. In fact, the freelancer can have as many clients as he can attract and cater to.

One more unique thing about freelancing is that you choose your own work hours. As a freelancer, you can freelance full time, part time or on a one-time basis only. Once you have been awarded a project, you also have the power to determine the nature of your work. In most cases, you get to choose your work hours (whether morning, afternoon or night), when to begin work, and where to work.

You are your own boss in a sense, when you freelance, but you are a boss who has many other employers (clients) who pay for your time and expertise in your field. As your own employer however, you (and not your clients) are responsible for your insurance and taxes.

The beautiful thing about freelancing is that once you have shown expertise in your chosen field, most clients do not care if you have a degree in that field or not, as they are more interested in demonstrable competence. Your clients are also not interested if you freelance full time or if you still hold down a nine-to-five job while taking on freelance jobs on the side. Clients want results and want you to deliver these results in a specified time. Once your skills match with the requirements required by the client, you are ready to go to work.

Freelance has become an acceptable, and sometimes envied, way to be employed and the freelance world is growing at such a high rate that it is now called the Gig Economy, and is now been considered as a new kind of labor market.

The great news is that nearly every type of service that most businesses need can be provided by a freelancer. This means that there are freelancing opportunities in the more obvious fields of writing, web page design and graphic design, as well as in the less obvious fields of accounting, marketing, project management, social media management, tutoring, virtual assistant etc.

While some freelancers focus on the general areas mentioned above, some focus on specific industries, and this is why you might find a freelancer who offers services as a real estate assistant, or as a political paper copywriter.

Income from freelancing can vary a lot and the rate at which you get paid depends on your experience, reviews, previous freelancing work history etc. The range of rates can be as little at $5 for a single project, to a recurring payment of potentially $100's of dollars per day for larger projects.

ADVANTAGES OF FREELANCING

Freelancing attracts freelancers mostly because it allows them to work from the comfort of their own homes, which means it effectively eliminates the hassle of starting every day early in order to be in the office at a specific time. Apart from this very obvious advantage, there are several other advantages to working as a freelancer. Here are some of them:

- **Flexible hours**: As a freelancer, you get to work whenever you want, choosing your schedule, and working at the time when you are most productive. This means that if you are the kind of person who is most productive at night or at other hours that are not considered regular, you get to work when you can get the most done in the shortest amount of time.
- **Autonomy to pick clients and job**: As a freelancer, you have the choice of picking the clients you want to work with and the jobs you want to work on. This is different from working in an office setting where you must work with whichever client your company gives you to work with and on whatever file you are assigned. However, it is important to note that you'll probably need to take smaller or less paying projects

initially until you've built up a reputation as a reputable and trusted freelancer.
- **Freedom to work wherever**: As a freelancer, you can work if you are in town or even when you go out of town (in most cases) as long as you are connected online. Since you don't have to be at a physical desk to complete your tasks, you have the freedom to work not only whenever you please, but also wherever you please. You can even take some work along on vacation if you are hard pressed for the cash. There have been instances though where freelancers has been asked to work at client sites due to security or when you have to interact with people.
- **You answer to yourself only**: When you freelance, you answer to only yourself and to an extent, your client. This means that you can work at your own pace and have the responsibility of making any tough decisions that need to be made concerning you and your business.
- **You get all the profits**: If you work for yourself as a freelancer, you get to keep all profits that you make on each job/project. This is quite different from when you work for a company and you get the same salary, no matter how big any project you work on is or how much your company is paid for that job.
- **You can achieve a better work-life balance**: As a freelancer, you eliminate the stress of commuting to and from work, and no longer have to hurry in order to catch the bus to get to work on time. This means that you can take care of other personal stuff that you need to without having to go through the same routine of work every day. This is why freelancing is such an attractive option for parents with children who want to work and at the same time want to be physically available to their children.
- **Freelancing breaks geographical barriers**: Freelan-

cing allows you to gain access to clients that are not in the same geographic area as you are. You can work for a client in a neighboring state or for a client who is halfway around the world. Being able to work beyond in this way allows you to work on what rewards your skill the best.

- **Faster growth opportunities**: As a freelancer, you have access to faster growth opportunities that a full-time job might not offer you. First, you get to develop and nurture your interpersonal skills and work on your ability to deal with different kinds of situations. You are exposed to various kinds of companies and domains and as a result can learn more in two years of freelancing than you would being in one or two jobs in that same period of time. As a freelancer, you start from scratch with any new client and have to build your own work portfolio in order to establish credibility. All this ends up making you a pre-sales person, a sales person, a marketing executive and a customer relationship officer.
- **The opportunity to push boundaries and experiment**: Most organizations have standard procedures on how to handle processes and situations, and most employees' creativity gets muzzled by these standards. Freelancing however gives you to opportunity to be as creative as you want and to truly experiment with your skill set. For example, a writer who works for a magazine might be constrained to a particular beat e.g. crime. As a freelance writer, this writer also has the opportunity to work on stuff such as legal writing, product descriptions, white papers, e books on a variety of topics, and so much more.
- **Easy and cheap to get started**: As long as you have the ability to provide a certain service, the start-up costs for starting a freelancing business is almost always relatively small. Signing up for most freelancing sites

are also relatively painless and you'll be able to offer your services in less time it would take you to make a coffee.
- **High demand**: A lot of companies no longer hire employees but depend on quality, reliable freelancers to get their business going. This is cheaper for these organizations as the overhead costs for running the business gets lower. A lot of these companies also pay top dollar for freelancers since they don't have to contend payroll fees or other employee benefits.
- **You might pay less in taxes**: This happens because the IRS mostly treats independent contractors and employees differently. For example, employees cannot deduct unreimbursed work-related expenses while independent contractors can.

THE DISADVANTAGES OF FREELANCING

As attractive as freelancing sounds, it is not perfect for everyone, as it has some guide for you to succeed. I've to include them in this chapter so you can be fully prepared. Knowing the challenge you might face and how to overcome them will make you a better and successful freelancer. Here are some of them:

- **You still have a schedule**: Because your clients have a time frame for their jobs to be completed, you also still have a schedule. While you have the opportunity to determine your own hours for the most part, you still need to work within deadlines.
- **Inconsistent work**: Freelance work, as popular as it has become, is not known for its consistency. If your niche in the freelance world is the delivery of one-off services, you might not always have work once you have turned over the finished product to your client. You will then need to find a new client who wants your product. This disadvantage can however be avoided, especially if you are a seasoned freelancer. Most freelancers who have experience doing what they do often find clients who have a substantial volume of consistent work, and work hard to impress these clients such that they become regular service

providers.
- **It won't make you rich overnight**: Freelance is often a long, hard journey despite its benefits of you being able to work at your own pace and at your own hours. Most freelancers see an ebb and flow in their work, and often have to plan for leaner times when the work is flowing. They also have to work hard to deliver jobs on time when the work is plentiful. This means that there are times when freelancer work even harder and more intensely than individuals who work at a nine to five job.
- **Client and project juggling:** You have to manage multiple clients and projects at the same time. While you may enjoy the variety of working on several projects at the same time, there are times when it becomes challenging to keep track of deadlines. To be a successful freelancer, you need to have good time management skills, be organized, and have the ability to pace yourself in order to produce and deliver quality work on time.
- **Jack of all trades:** You are your own manager, bookkeeper, public relations officer etc. As a freelancer, you are responsible for all aspects of your freelancing career. This means that you are responsible for invoicing, marketing bookkeeping, and dealing with difficult clients etc. There is simply no other person to hide behind, so you will be forced to develop more skills than just the basic ability to do the work you're freelancing.
- **Difficulty separating personal and work time**: Because a higher workload means higher earnings, freelancers often have difficulty separating work time from personal time. You are your own boss, can work in any location and at any time. It thus becomes challenging to recognize and separate personal life and work time. More often than not, this often defeats

the original purpose of freelancing which is to have more personal and family time.
- **Freelancing requires a lot of research**: You will need to become a research pro to become successful at freelancing, as you will need to acquire more knowledge in your chosen field.
- **Risk of not being paid**: As a freelancer, you face the risk of not getting paid for a completed job that you gave your everything to. There is no freelancer alive that has not experienced this. Even if you get your work from a reliable source, you still face this risk.
- **No employer benefits**: Most freelancers do not have health benefits and other employer benefits such as maternity leave. If you need a health cover as a freelancer, you need to get one yourself. If you want to add to or begin your retirement savings, you will need to do this yourself. If you are pregnant, you either continue work through your pregnancy and immediately after your child is born if you are to continue earning from freelancing.
- **Self-employment tax**: When you work for a company, your employer pays half of your Medicare and Social Security taxes. When you work for yourself, you will have to pay both halves.
- **A new set of constraints**: While working from the comfort of your own home is often cited as an attractive feature of freelancing, working from home brings with it a new set of constraints, particularly for married women with families. More often than not, women who freelance continue to bear the brunt of child care and household chores despite increases in paid work time.

GETTING STARTED AS A FREELANCER

If you have decided to become a freelancer because you have skills that you can offer to potential clients, whether from your past employment experience or using talents that you already have, there are seven basic steps that you must take to give yourself a higher probability of success in the freelance world.

- **Definition of goals**: Why do you want to freelance? Is it because you want to earn extra income asides the one you already earn from your regular job? Is it because you want to be your own boss? Is it so that you can have more time for family and friends? While there is no right or wrong reason for wanting to become a freelancer, it is very important to be clear about your reason. It is important to note that all of the world's top entrepreneurs agree that there must be a clear and unambiguous definition of goals to successfully start any endeavor.
- **Find a niche that is profitable.** No matter the discipline you choose to freelance in, there will be thousands, if not hundreds of thousands of other freelancers offering the same services at a price lower than yours. This means that you must get over the idea of trying to compete on the basis of price. Instead, find a

profitable niche for your freelance business and compete on the basis of value, not price. For example, you don't have to take any graphic design project that comes your way if you are a freelance graphic designer. You might want to concentrate instead exclusively on eBook layouts. As a freelance writer, you might want to specialize in white papers rather than on all kinds of writing.

- **Identify the right clients:** You not only need to find a profitable niche, but the right clients as well. Make a list of the kind of client you want to work with, target clients that fall within this category and pursue them first. After working with a few of them, you will have a very clear sense of whether or not you want to continue pursuing similar clients.
- **Set your prices strategically:** If you are to be successful as a freelance, you need to price yourself based on the value you can deliver, and not based on what your competitors charge or the money that you need to fund your lifestyle. The truth of the matter is that there is nothing like prices that are too high if you deliver the right value. So, if you are sure about your value delivery, don't be afraid to charge top dollar for your work. It might not be easy initially, but you will eventually find clients who are willing to pay a premium rate for jobs well done. If you are however not confident about the value you can deliver, don't make your clients pay through their noses for your services. If you do, you won't have repeat customers. To better enter the market, I'd suggest also to do some research to find out the market rates for your skill set.
- **Make examples of what you can deliver:** If you have a website, let it be a place to demonstrate your expertise. Create examples of the exact type of services you offer and display (if possible) on your website. If

you are a freelance writer, your target client should be able to read content written and published by you on your website. If you're a web designer, your site should be very accurately curated since it is a representation of what can build for your clients.

- **Mention target clients in your content:** Be specific by regularly mentioning the brands, persons and companies that you see yourself potentially working with one day.
- **Learn how to pitch yourself:** Knowing how to pitch yourself is an important part of freelancing. Because you are your own boss and have no advertisement team backing you, generating new business is your responsibility and yours alone. Learn therefore how to communicate the strengths that you have.

WHAT YOU NEED TO KNOW ABOUT FREELANCING

When you work at a paid job in an organization, most of the money stuff that concerns you is automatically taken care of by your organization. You get your salary at the end of the month without having to demand for it. You have your taxes automatically deducted, your retirement contribution automatically deducted, and your insurance taken care of. You simply get a payment at the end of the month that you know is yours for spending (or saving).

Things are a little different when you earn a living through freelancing. Here are some important points to consider before going the freelance route:
- **Your taxes**: While your taxes are not deducted automatically as an independent contractor, that doesn't mean you do not have to pay them. Depending on the country that you're from, you might need to fill out a tax form when you sign on with a new freelance client, so that your client can report what he paid you to the government. On your part, you will need keeping track of your earnings in the year, and determine by yourself roughly how much you owe in taxes. You

will then make an estimated tax payment on a quarterly basis. Always make sure that you send in the right amount, and you need to know that not paying your estimated quarterly taxes can lead to tax penalties from the various government agencies in your country. As a business owner, any expenses incurred as part of your operations can be deducted from your taxable income. This can include your Internet service or home office deductions such as some of your mortgage and utilities if you work from home.

- **Insurance and other benefits:** You're on your own for benefits which includes health insurance and retirement planning if you're a full-time freelancer. You will need to purchase your own health insurance and set up your own retirement account and then ensure that you fund these accounts appropriately. This can be hard to do because of the inconsistency of the income that comes from freelancing.
- **Getting paid:** Getting paid for your services is often the most frustrating and time-consuming aspect of freelancing. This is why it is important to have a contract that specifies the terms of your engagement when you begin a new gig with a new client. This contract should specify the deliverables and the compensation. Some clients have a standard contract for their vendors and service providers, but you might need to draw one up yourself if your new client doesn't. You will most likely have to negotiate before getting to a mutually agreed upon compensation. This is because some companies have a standard rate they pay to their contractors; while you as a contractor might have a standard rate that you charge clients. If your numbers and your new client's own are far apart, you should be prepared to negotiate, as well as ready to walk away if they don't meet your standard. Getting paid after your work is done

will also mean sending in an invoice or fulfilling the client's standards for getting paid. Bear in mind that there will always be dud clients who will not want to pay at all or pay in full or in time, so you need to have a system in place for getting these kinds of payment.
- **Using the internet:** The Internet has opened up so many freelance opportunities for freelancers, and it is now commonplace to be physically resident in an African country or India and be working on a job you got from a client resident in the United States through an online platform connecting business owners and freelancers. The internet now provides economical access to remote workers as freelance marketplaces provide a platform for both freelancers and buyers. Freelancers can create a profile where they include a description of the services they offer, information about their rates and examples of their work. On the other hand, buyers register and complete a basic profile, and then post projects outlining their requirements. This means that there are more opportunities for freelancing than there were fifteen years ago. If you have tried to freelance on your own and have not made any headway, you might want to consider registering as a freelancer on one of these freelance marketplaces. We will examine these marketplaces one by one in a later chapter.

BEST WEBSITES FOR GENERAL FREELANCE SERVICES

These freelance websites have a general sampling of freelance jobs. It doesn't matter if you are a writer, marketer, designer, developer, salesperson, photographer or any other service provider, you will find freelance jobs on these platforms:

- **Fiverr**: This is one of the more popular general service freelance platforms. Every job here starts at $5, and while this may sound low, it is very easy to set your tiers above the base $5 option.
- **Upwork:** This is also one of the more popular freelance platforms, formed by the merger of oDesk and Elance, two very powerful platforms for landing freelance jobs. Upwork has over 5 million clients and 12 million freelancers. and lists upwards of 3 million freelance jobs each year. If you are prepared to take lower priced jobs, Upwork is the way to begin because it has such a large client base but also takes a 20% cut until you have built up a regular relationship with a client.
- **CloudPeeps:** This platform allows you to begin on a higher pay level than Fiverr and Upwork does. This is

a great site for you if you already have a great portfolio and have the experience to begin at a higher level. It's a bit harder to join CloudPeeps though, but you can get jobs easily once you've been accepted.
- **College Recruiter:** If you are a recent grad or a student looking for freelance jobs on a part time basis, College Recruiter gives you the opportunity to get a great beginner job through which you can garner experience and contacts for future work.
- **Freelancer:** Freelancer has a huge variety of projects to offer freelancers. You get eight free applications before you must pay a membership fee. It is a popular website because it has one of the cheaper commission rates.
- **Guru:** Guru charges a 9% commission and makes it very easy to create a profile that highlights your experience. You can also go through all the job postings made every day once you have created a profile.
- **ServiceScape:** ServiceScape is a global platform catering to freelancers with a variety of skills and experience. While it allows anyone from any service industry to register and get jobs, it places an emphasis on writing, editing, graphic design, and translating. It currently boasts of more than 259,000 completed projects and 79,000 satisfied clients.
- **FlexJobs**: FlexJobs sorts freelance jobs and remote and otherwise flexible gigs industry by industry. One advantage of using FlexJobs is that it thoroughly researches jobs and monitors new gigs pretty carefully.
- **SolidGigs:** SolidGigs is one of the easier and more convenient and time saving platforms to use. Instead of you spending hours every week searching through new freelance jobs, the team at SolidGigs curates and goes through all freelance job boards and sends you the top 2% of freelance gigs from around the web

every single week. This means that you don't have to do the time-consuming work of filtering through dozens of freelance job boards yourself.

BEST WEBSITES FOR GRAPHICS DESIGNER FREELANCE SERVICES

If you are a designer, here are the best websites for freelance:

- **Angel List:** All kinds of companies, from start-ups to well established ones, search for design talent on Angel List. It is a great place for designers to get noticed.
- **Art Wanted:** This website puts an emphasis on graphic designers and digital illustrators. All you need to do is register and then put samples of your work on your profile page. Clients browse through works by keywords, and will contact you if your artwork or illustration catches their attention.
- **Envato Studio:** This website offers a platform for all kinds of graphics designers but if logos are your bread and butter, register on Envato Studio ASAP because it gives logo designers a kind of a VIP treatment. The platform is very easy to use and has a very fast turnaround.
- **Coroflot:** This platform acts as a matchmaker between design artists and clients. As a freelancer, you post your portfolio while clients post the project

they need. Coroflot then acts as the go-between, and sets up connections between you and the client.
- **Smashing Magazine:** This platform is a great resource for both designers and developers, as long as you are prepared to sort through the postings by yourself.
- **CrowdSPRING:** This website caters to designers and all other kinds of creatives, encompassing all sorts of design i.e. from logo design to general graphics design. It is a free platform for freelancers to sign up on and is very easy to use.
- **Working Not Working:** This is a very exclusive platform, accepting only a minute proportion of the applicants wanting to join the platform. It was founded by two former freelancers who have had the opportunity to work with the very best clients in the field of design. It is a difficult platform to get accepted into, but once accepted, you can get gigs from client companies such as Apple, Facebook, and Google at top dollar rates.

BEST PLATFORMS FOR WEBSITE AND SOFTWARE DEVELOPING SERVICES

These websites provide work for freelance designers and website developers:

- **YouTeam**: YouTeam is a phenomenal platform that will set you up with remote contract work and freelance jobs on-demand if you're an experienced software developer. Not all the engineers on this platform are full-time freelancers, but it is a great place to find some long-term projects if you're already a developer for another IT consulting firm. This platform places an emphasis on vetting and verifying software firms and their developers, and this adds another layer of credibility to the website.
- **Codeable**: This is a platform that gives WordPress experts a forum to do their thing and make money, focusing on offering clients everything from WordPress themes to plugins expertise. If you are not a WordPress expert, don't bother signing up.
- **Gun.io**: Gun.io offers freelancers the opportunity to land gigs from companies such as Zappos, Tesla, and Cisco. It is also one of the best freelancing platforms

because it thoroughly vets companies that hire freelancers, as well as the remote developers applying to get gigs on the platform.
- **Lorem**: Lorem is on the rise as one of the best destinations to get short-term freelance jobs that focus on designing, building and fixing websites. It is very appealing to freelancers because there is no monthly fee to be able to list freelance jobs. Most gigs pay between $25 and $250.
- **Joomlancer**: Joomlancer is a great place for tech wizards, as it has a very fast sign up process. What more, you can immediately start bidding on jobs once signed up. The focus is on intermediate to advanced software projects, so beginners cannot really benefit from this platform.
- **Rent a Coder**: On this platform, clients looking for programmers, designers and developers are linked with freelancers offering the said services. Signing up for freelancers is free.
- **10x Management**: This platform allows all kinds of tech freelancers to sign up and offer their services, everything from website developers to cybersecurity gurus. If you have a niche tech specialty, this is a great platform to be on.
- **Gigster**: Gigster is a great platform for web designers, software designers, and app developers. Gigster has a tough screening process that makes it hard to get accepted. The upside is that Gigster uses AI to match freelancers with projects.
- **Programmer Meet Designer**: This platform brings together all kinds of freelancers, from programmers, to developers, and designers. It's quite an easy job board to search through, as it highlights client's budget, the deadline and the skill set required.

BEST PLATFORMS FOR CUSTOMER SUPPORT SERVICES

Do you know you can also offer your services as a customer support person remotely? If you have skills to offer in terms of customer support and relationships and are interested in freelancing, check out these websites:

- **We Work Remotely:** While this website is for freelancers of all types, it focuses more on customer support jobs. You will however need to sacrifice the time needed to sift through all the postings on the site to find what suits you.
- **Virtual Vocations:** As with We Work Remotely, you will also need to sacrifice the time needed to sift through all the postings on the Virtual Vocations site to find what suits you.
- **Support Driven:** This website offers freelancers the opportunity to offer business and customer support services from the comforts of their homes.

BEST PLATFORMS FOR MARKETERS

A marketer has excellent spoken and written communication skills, is a creative and open-minded person who is able and willing to change his marketing approach every now and then, and someone who has strong organizational and planning abilities, and great team leadership qualities. A good marketer is able to drive processes and can motivate others to see the end goal while working on day-to-day tasks.

Marketers of all kinds can find work in almost all the big freelance marketplaces, so feel free to check all the general services websites like Upwork and Guru. However, there are some platforms that specialize in finding freelance gigs for marketers. Here are some of them:

- **Aquent**: Aquent is a great company makes marketing freelance connections for marketers. Aquent's clients specify the marketing gaps they need to fill, and Aquent turns to its group of freelancers to get the job done. Aquent focuses solely on marketing, but also offer gigs for freelancers in the tech and creative job fields as well.
- **People Per Hour**: This platform is a great one for mar-

keters, as well software engineers and SEO experts. Browsing through job opportunities on People Per Hour is free, and you can send out 15 free applications before you will be charged for sending out subsequent applications.

- **Remotive**: This is a standard job board that has many categories and allows you to search them for free. It has a really booming marketing category where you can easily see what job is posted, its location, and what specialty within marketing that it falls under.

THE BEST PLATFORMS FOR VIDEO EDITING SERVICES

We are all aware that technology and the advent of high-resolution mobile phones has made videography a lot more accessible than it used to be. However, while anyone can hold an iPhone vertically and press video record, it is not everyone that can put together a polished looking video out of their footage. If you are good at video editing (By which I mean the process of manipulating and rearranging video shots in a way that a new work is created. Video editing in this way is considered as just one part of the post production process with other post-production tasks including titling, colour correction, sound mixing), you can get jobs from these video editing platforms:

- **Assemble.tv**: This is a highly curated network of video creatives including copywriters, creative directors, directors, motion artists, photographers, editors, and many more. Assemble works with recognizable brands and connects them with top creative talent, so it makes sure that its pool of creative talent is thoroughly screened. If you are sure that you can pass Assemble's stringent quality standards, go ahead and apply.
- **Production Hub**: Production Hub is a video editing marketplace that focuses exclusively on media pro-

duction. The basic plan is about $5 a month, but there are great jobs to be had here.
- **Stage 32**: Stage 32 works like a job board while also functioning like a networking site. You can look through video editing jobs posted, and apply for the ones you can do. Word of mouth also allows good video editors go far on this platform. This means that you can get jobs through the job board, as well as through referrals.
- **Behance**: Behance posts video editing jobs regularly that you can apply for if you are registered on the platform. The website is very user friendly and they make it easy for freelancers to put together a great portfolio so that clients can find them.
- **Mandy**: Mandy focuses only on film and TV production work. If you do video editing for other purposes, don't bother applying. If you work in film and TV though, this is fantastic news for you, as you don't have to sort through irrelevant jobs. The disadvantage however is that you're competing for the same jobs with other people who offer the exact same services that you do. This means that you have to do all that you can to stand out with a polished portfolio.

THE BEST PLATFORMS FOR SALES

What do effective sales people have in character that others do not? How about the ability to listen, knowing how to feel what their customers feel, having a need to sell that goes beyond the money, competitiveness, a great networking ability, confidence, resiliency and enthusiasm?

If you have these attributes, congratulations; you can sell ice to an eskimo. But beyond being an effective salesperson and selling stuff to people, can you sell yourself? If you can, why not head off to these marketplaces to find a freelance sales position?

- **Red Hat**: Red Hat employs freelancers and remote workers on behalf of their higher-level clients. These freelancers do any and everything from sales to software development. If you are a great salesperson, why not give it a try?
- **Salesforce App Exchange Job Board**: Salesforce is better known as a leading customer relationship management tool for all kinds of companies. It however also has an App Exchange job board where companies that do business with Salesforce can post about their hiring needs. Many freelancers have found remote

sales positions this way.
- **ZipRecruiter**: Many companies use ZipRecruiter not just to hire full-time talent, but also to advertise for high-quality freelance jobs with opportunities to do part-time sales for top companies. If you are accepted into the very elite company of ZipRecruiter freelancers, you can earn anything between $500 and $10,000 per month, but what you earn will be dependent on the company, your skill set, and your experience. Some companies pay a part-time salary as well as commission on sales, while some do only a part time salary and some only do commission.
- **Skip the Drive**: Skip the Drive is a general job board website, but it has a lot of sales jobs posted on it. Skip the Drive has a humorous side to it, and it tells freelancers just how much they saved by not driving or making the commute to the office.

THE BEST PLATFORMS FOR PHOTOGRAPHER SERVICES

If you are great with a camera and can get angles and views like no other person you know, perhaps it is time to use your photography skills to earn a little money on the side. If you are interested in photography freelancing, here are some websites to check out:

- **Photography Jobs Central**: Creative Jobs Central is the parent company of Photography Jobs Central, which is a fairly typical freelance photography marketplace. This is a good opportunity for serious minded photographers. While the premium membership does cost a pretty sum, the platform also has more than a thousand actively posting companies. This means that you have a guarantee of clinching photography jobs in your area. What more, the platform works hard to weed out amateurs and thus gives skilled photographers less competition in a bid to get profitable work.
- **Craigslist**: Craigslist actually is a general services freelance marketplace, but it has a special niche for photographers. The website is a classified ads website that has sections that focus on jobs, for sale, items wanted, housing, services, résumés, community service, gigs, and discussion forums. The need for

photography comes from businesses and individuals looking to build up their portfolio. You can be that freelance photographer that photographs these portfolios and gets paid for it. The catch is that while you can book jobs online, you will have to physically go to the site of the job to complete your task.
- **Airbnb**: Airbnb employs freelance photographers and sends them on home visits in order to photograph the homes registered on the site. This is why the platform can boldly state that the photos on their site are verified. All you need to do is to check if Airbnb is hiring in your region and then apply accordingly. The good news is that Airbnb often gives fantastic photographers repeat jobs.
- **Photography Jobs Finder**: If you are trying to find photography jobs, why not head off to Photography Jobs Finder? Photography Jobs Finder is a job board in which you can search through all the photography jobs posted by clients. You can also upload your resume so that clients can find you.
- **Photography Jobs Online**: Photography Jobs Online works a little bit differently than other photography job boards. Here, you upload your photos and see if someone wants to buy one or some of them. So, you are not being hired for a new job per se, but you are uploading your pictures to see if anyone is interested in purchasing them. This is a good avenue to make money if you have an accumulation of pictures that you want to try and make money from.
- **Journalism Jobs**: Journalism jobs is a freelance marketplace for both journalists and photojournalists. Because every great story needs a good picture to go with it, this is a good place to get started if you're planning to go into the photojournalism field.
- **Freelance Photographer Jobs**: Freelance Photographer Jobs is an aggregate job platform of photog-

raphy postings from around the internet. It is a curated website, so this means that they have verified most of the jobs that are posted.

Francois Hensley

THE BEST WEBSITES FOR WRITING FREELANCE JOBS

Do you weave magic with your words and wrap the reader in your sensational sentences (if you do fiction), or do your words motivate your reader to get up and go do the very thing you ask of them (if you do sales or motivational writing)?

If you have the ability to communicate with your reader beyond just your written words, and have a fantastic knowledge of grammar, spelling, and punctuation, your writing skills might just very well become a money maker for you.

Perhaps you have been trying to earn money with your writing while working at a regular job before now but have not been so successful. Here are quite a number of freelance writing platforms that might need your services and pay top dollar for it:

- **Contena**: If you are looking for sheer volume of high quality and well-paid jobs as a writer, an editor and a content creator of any kind, look no further than Contena. This great resource features a mix of full-time remote jobs and freelance jobs on its platform. You will find adverts for freelance writing jobs such as a sports writing position, an eBook gig for a tech publication, or photography-focused content writing jobs. There is something for every writer here, from jobs that pay as little as $25 to jobs that pay as much as $10,000 per month. I like to call Contena the writing freelance platform for the serious-minded freelance writer.

- **Freelance Writing Gigs**: Freelance Writing Gigs is a very well curated job board that is updated every day from Monday to Friday with new jobs and new clients. You can always check back every single day on the job board and find a writing gig that might be very worth your while.
- **PubLoft**: If you are client shy and never want to relate directly with a client, but still yearn for great freelance writing opportunities, PubLoft is the place for you. You will find well paid freelance jobs for clients that are reliable without ever needing to interact directly with the clients. Once you have demonstrated your writing competence, PubLoft will handle client management and help you find good work. Actually, PubLoft's promise is that freelancers who sign up with them never have to find, sell, or manage another customer again. If you manage to get on PubLoft's freelance list, you can start smiling to the bank with rates starting at $150 per post.
- **Contently**: Contently is a platform of many parts. It is first a free portfolio for creative freelancers. It is also an online publication that offers great freelance advice. Finally, it is also a great platform for getting freelance jobs with very successful brands. These freelance jobs include writing gigs. You must first create a portfolio, and if your portfolio catches the eye, you will be selected by Contently's account management team. This team then manages your writing skill in an agency style and connects you directly with well-paying clients for very well-paid freelance

writing projects. Projects range between $600 – $1,600 per article depending on the scope and length of the project.
- **Blogging Pro**: While its name may suggest that this marketplace focuses only on blogging, it doesn't. It is a full on writing freelance market where you can find tasks as simple as helping people to begin their blogs to tasks as complex as ghost writing and general copywriting. The platform works by aggregating good writing jobs sourced from the internet, and you can browse through the writing jobs for free to see if there is any that matches your competency.
- **Journalism Jobs**: Journalism jobs is a freelance marketplace for both journalists and photojournalists. It curates journalism gigs from around the web but also offers freelance writers the opportunity to work on other mainstream writing, as well as editing gigs.
- **Morning Coffee Newsletter**: When you sign up for Morning Coffee Newsletter (which is free and very easy to do), you receive an email every single day with news about the greatest and latest freelance writing jobs. It is a great help for beginner writers who can't seem to find any other helpful resource.
- **Freelance Writing**: Freelance Writing has something for every writer, no matter your skill and experience. Whether you are a very skilled writer with years and years of experience under your belt or whether you are a newly minted writer, as long as you have writing skills, you will find something for you here. You can filter the type of job you want to do by the experience you have.

THE BEST WEBSITES FOR VIRTUAL ASSISTANTS

If you are great at research, data entry, bookkeeping, and answering emails professionally, you can get work as a freelance or remote virtual assistant on the following sites:

- **Belay**: Belay is a platform that connects clients to virtual personal assistant. The work is always remote, so you don't have to be physically present at the client's location. You have nothing to lose by checking if the platform has any openings in your specialty.
- **Zirtual**: Zirtual offers virtual assistants the opportunity to work full time but remotely. The platform hires freelance virtual assistants on a full-time basis for various specialties. One unique thing about this platform is that it actually has an employer/employee relationship with freelancers and is one of the very few platforms that has employee benefits for its workers.
- **Fancy Hands**: Fancy Hands hires freelancers to provide services ranging from data entry to phone calls for its clients, and parse out services by task, which are worth various dollar amounts. There are even managerial positions available on Fancy Hands.
- **Worldwide 101**: Worldwide 101 is a bit more "pre-

mium" than other matching services. The virtual assistants on this platform get more regular work and work with clients who are generally higher end, and who pay more. The best way to impress Worldwide 101 enough to get on its list of freelancers is to be well experienced, as well as some other special skill e.g speaking another language.
- **Time Etc**: Time Etc is a fantastic platform if you are looking to land freelance gigs as a virtual assistant. The platform has only once focus, and that is on the virtual assistant space. This means that you will definitely find a virtual assistant gig here if you check back consistently for new updates.
- **ClickWorker**: If you are an expert in the fields of data entry, writing, and researching, ClickWorker is looking for you. The platform caters to a variety of clients, small and big, and it's a great way to get started as a virtual assistant. All you need to do is take a quick assessment test to get access to the jobs board.
- **Amazon Mechanical Turk**: You can find work very easily and very quickly on Amazon Mechanical Turk. The process is so easy that you could very well be on your first job one hour after completing the registration. This is because the platform always has a lot of virtual assistant-type work available. You need to know though that most of these jobs are not well paid. If you are very experienced and place a premium on your skills, this may not be the platform for you. It is however a great place to start for newbies.
- **VA Networking**: You can network with other virtual assistants on VA Networking, as well have the access to its job board. The website also offers great advice and fantastic resources for beginner virtual assistants, so it is a great place to begin if you are a newbie.
- **Assistant Match**: Assistant Match directly matches freelance virtual assistants with available opportun-

ities. This means that you do not need to comb through a job board. When you register on the platform, you will give information on your skills, and this is what Assistant Match uses to match you up with what its clients need. While the pay isn't so great for beginners, one great thing about Assistant Match is that it offers training for areas in which you may be lacking as a virtual assistant.

CONCLUSION

If you have decided that the freelance life is for you, and are serious about earning a living from freelancing, congratulations. I believe that the wealth of information that you have gathered from this book will prompt you to work harder at honing your craft and will provide the encouragement that you need at the times that things don't seem to be going in your favor.

At this point, it is important to remind ourselves once again of the many benefits of freelancing. They, once again, are:

- Flexible hours: Getting to work whenever you want, choosing your schedule, and working at the time when you are most productive.
- Autonomy to pick clients and job: Having the choice of picking the clients you want to work with and the jobs you want to work on.
- Freedom to work wherever: Working whether you are in town or out of town.
- You answer to yourself only, and not an employer.
- You get all the profits when you work for yourself as a freelancer.
- You can achieve a better work-life balance by eliminating the stress of commuting to and from work, and no longer have to hurry in order to catch the bus to

get to work on time. This means that you can take care of other personal stuff that you need to without having to go through the same routine of work every day.
- Freelancing breaks geographical barriers and allows you to gain access to clients that are not in the same geographic area as you are.
- Faster growth opportunities because you get to develop and nurture your interpersonal skills and work on your ability to deal with different kinds of situations.
- Easy to get started, as long as you have the ability to provide a certain service.
- It is in high demand.

Now, that we've reminded ourselves of just what benefits freelance offers, make sure that you sit down to do your very own research before heading off into freelance. Find out if the skills and experience you have is marketable. If it is not, you will need to first work on honing your skills and growing yourself professionally. There are many resources online that will help you hone your craft, no matter what that craft is.

Use this book as a launching pad to thoroughly research the freelance websites that best suit your purposes. Who knows, you might just be able to kick that nine-to-five job for good and live the freelancer lifestyle.

See you at the top!

www.ingramcontent.com/pod-product-compliance
Lightning Source LLC
Chambersburg PA
CBHW070840220526
45466CB00002B/837